Critical Strategic Decisions in Mexico: the Future of US/Mexican Defense Relations

by Dr. Richard D. Downie

Center for Hemispheric Defense Studies

Strategic Issues in US/Latin American Relations
CHDS Occasional Paper
July 2011 Volume 1 Number 1
Series Editor: Dr. Howard J. Wiarda

Contents

Preface

With this study on the future of US/Mexico defense relations, we inaugurate the new Occasional Papers Series on strategic issues in US/Latin American relations at the Center for Hemispheric Defense Studies (CHDS). This new series is part of an ambitious new agenda of research, conferences, publications, and outreach launched by CHDS.

This paper not only initiates our new series, it also features an outstanding paper by CHDS Director, Dr. Richard Downie. Dr. Downie earned his Ph.D. at the University of Southern California in International Relations; his career has bridged military service, academics, and administration. Dr. Downie is an acknowledged expert on Latin America, military security, and Mexico.

In this paper, Dr. Downie first focuses on the history of US/Mexico security relations, emphasizing their longtime distant but now changing parameters. He traces the recent improvement in defense relations to President Felipe Calderón's decision to confront militarily Mexico's trained criminal organizations. His assessment points to a maturing yet still fragile relationship.

Beyond proving useful history lessons, Downie's thoughtful study concludes with an analysis of the potential options for critical strategic decisions involving Mexico and the United States. These several options are explored analytically and systematically, based on the author's thorough knowledge of Mexico as well as his insider's knowledge of US/Mexico strategic relations. His recommendations merit close attention by scholars as well as policymakers.

The paper provides not just a rich and stimulating analysis but serves as an excellent introduction to our new series. We are pleased to provide a copy to you.

Howard J. Wiarda
Professor of National Security Policy
Associate Director for Research and Publications

The author offers special thanks to Mick Andersen, Jay Cope, Alfredo Corchado, Patricia Escamilla-Hamm, Erik Kjonnerod, Abraham Lowenthal, Bruce McClintock, Celina Realuyo, Rick Taylor, and Howard Wiarda for reviewing, providing valuable insights and commenting on this article. Whatever errors remain are my own.

Executive Summary

Mexican President Felipe Calderón's decision in 2006 to use the military (vs. the police) in the lead role to combat transnational criminal organizations (TCOs) and to cooperate with the US in that effort resulted in the best US/Mexican military-to-military and defense relations in decades. In many ways, this positive defense interaction serves as a visible bellwether for the level of each nation's commitment to jointly confront the TCOs. Will this level of cooperation and collaboration continue? The answer depends on a critical strategic decision the next president of Mexico must make after taking office in December 2013: What strategy will Mexico adopt to address the TCO threat?

This paper delineates four options that represent the range of possibilities available to the next president. These include:

A. Maintain the Calderón administration's current approach.
B. Place law enforcement (vs. the military) in the lead role in confronting the TCOs.
C. Adopt socially focused alternatives to address the societal causes underpinning Mexico's culture of lawlessness and impunity.
D. Accommodate or negotiate with the TCOs.

Spectrum of Mexico's Strategies to Counter TCO Threats: Options by Relative Levels of Collaboration

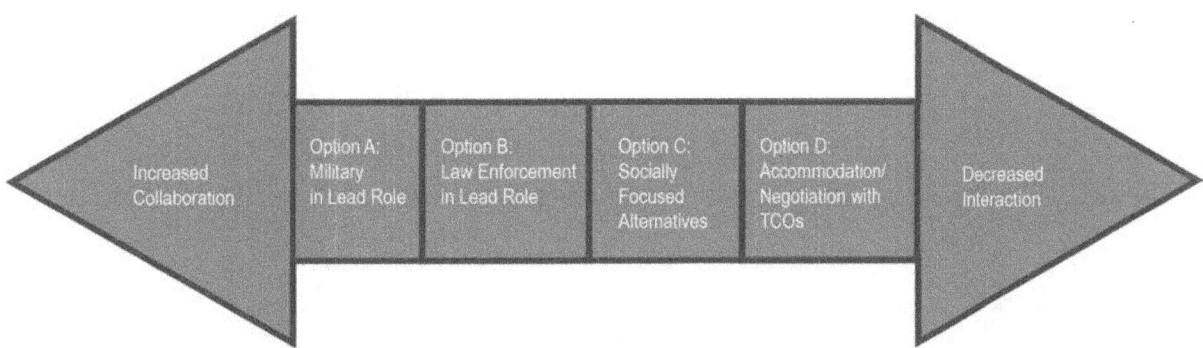

Each option offers distinctly different potential consequences for the future of the US/Mexico Defense relationship.

From a US perspective, Mexico's choice of an option that favors continued defense collaboration is preferable. Yet our policy has not demonstrated the necessary level of urgency or emphasis to highlight that our combined efforts are necessary to successfully confront the ominous challenge of transnational crime. The United States still has the opportunity to shape the conditions that may determine Mexico's strategic decisions.

The following recommendations are offered to help improve US/Mexican military-to-military and defense relations and mitigate the impact of potentially negative future political decisions:

- Demonstrate success during a rapidly closing "Window of Opportunity."
- Facilitate programs and actions that offer continuity in enhancing the US/Mexico defense relationship.
- Extend and institutionalize existing US/Mexican defense linkages and organizational arrangements.
- Coordinate a comprehensive US strategy that integrates with and demonstrates solidarity and support for Mexican efforts in confronting organized crime.
- Identify realistically attainable objectives and manage expectations.

Critical Strategic Decisions in Mexico: the Future of US/Mexican Defense Relations

1. Introduction

His Excellency Arturo Sarukhan, Ambassador of Mexico to the United States, visits with General Gene Renuart, NORAD and USNORTHCOM commander.

When General Gene Renuart, then Commander of the US Northern Command, highlighted in February 2010, that US/Mexican defense relations are better today than they have ever been, longtime observers were the most surprised of all.[1] The Mexican military has had frosty relations toward their US counterparts for decades. So the magnitude of this positive change in US/Mexican military-to-military relations in as little as four years raised a number of questions. What inspired this rapid improvement? Would US/Mexican defense relations continue to advance?[2] At that time, some US and Mexican military officials who had experienced this transformation believed that the "genie was out of the bottle" and that the relationship could never return to its traditional state. Another perspective indicated that the current warming trend might be an aberration, a temporary "marriage of convenience" in the formal, distant stance that has traditionally characterized the US/Mexican defense relationship. Based on such views, the overarching question is whether institutional factors or political decisions at the national level are more likely to determine the future outcome of the US/Mexican defense relationship.

---

1 General Victor "Gene" Renuart, Commander US Northern Command, comment made during presentation at the VMI, Woodrow Wilson Center Conference, Washington, D.C., March 2010.
2 Two recent articles are particularly helpful in framing the debate on these two questions: the history of the US-Mexico defense relationship, and the potentially paradigmatic change that occurred after the Calderón administration took office in December 2007. The first of these, entitled, "US-Mexico Defense Relations: An Incompatible Interface" (by Craig Deare, *Strategic Forum* [July 2009], no. 234, http://www.ndu.edu/inss), highlights historical difficulties underpinning US/Mexican defense relations. The other, by Gen Victor Renuart and Dr. Biff Baker, entitled, "US Mexico Mil-Mil Relations: A Compatible Interface" (*Strategic Forum* [February 2010], no. 243, http://www.ndu.edu/inss) is a response to Deare's article. Both make interesting and useful points. Obviously, future changes in the US/Mexico defense relationship reflect the validity of their analysis.

7

More recent tensions in US/Mexican relations may have helped answer some of those questions. Nevertheless, a key determinant will involve strategic decisions the next president of Mexico will make regarding his or her administration's strategy to address Transnational Criminal Organizations (TCOs). This article discusses the range of options available to the next president of Mexico and the impact each could have on the US/Mexican defense relationship. Those options range from: A. "Staying the current course"; B. "Changing to a police vs. military lead role against the TCOs"; C. "Adopting socially focused alternatives"; to D. "Accommodating or negotiating with the TCOs." Each of these presents unique advantages or challenges for the United States and would shape the interaction of defense and security forces between the two countries differently. Indeed, the President of Mexico's strategic decision will determine whether engagement between the two militaries—and between our countries—continues to improve or deteriorate.

To address these issues, this article first summarizes the thorny history of the US/Mexican defense relationship, including dramatic improvements and setbacks since the inauguration of President Felipe Calderón of Mexico. The second section assesses the gamut of potential options regarding the future of Mexico's strategy to fight against organized crime and derives potential consequences for future US/Mexico defense relations for each scenario.[3] These options range from continuation of the current approach to alternatives that would significantly shift the way Mexico deals with the TCOs. The final section offers recommendations regarding actions that could demonstrate US commitment to a combined effort with Mexico, foster enhanced defense relations, and mitigate a return to strained defense relations.

2. Historical Context: The "Distant" and Changing US/Mexico Defense Relationship

A Mexican security analyst commented recently that the current level of US/Mexican military cooperation would have seemed inconceivable in 2005.[4] Implicitly, that statement highlights both the past estrangement and the significant change that has occurred in the US/Mexico defense relationship. With some notable exceptions, the Mexican military's approach to their US counterparts has for decades largely been stiff and formal. Mexico's military leadership has been wary of bilateral engagement beyond a limited set of routine meetings and events. That situation is understandable, considering the history of past US military interventions into Mexico and, more importantly, that the mission of Mexico's armed forces is to defend their sovereign territory. Given this foundation of Mexican reluctance and resistance to military-to-military involvement, the level of US/Mexican engagement in defense issues over the past five years is particularly surprising.

---

3 Countries have a variety of political, economic, social as well as defense, security, and other elements through which to influence the actions of another state. This paper holds constant the impact of other variables to examine the cause-and-effect relationship between the options discussed and potential consequences regarding the US/Mexico relationship.

4 Dr. Abelardo Rodríguez Sumano, November 8, 2010, Mexico City, Mexico.

8

July 2011 Volume 1 Number 1
Strategic Issues in U.S.-Latin American Relations
Critical Strategic Decisions in Mexico: the Future of US/Mexican Defense Relations

The Annexation of Northern Mexico 1845–1848

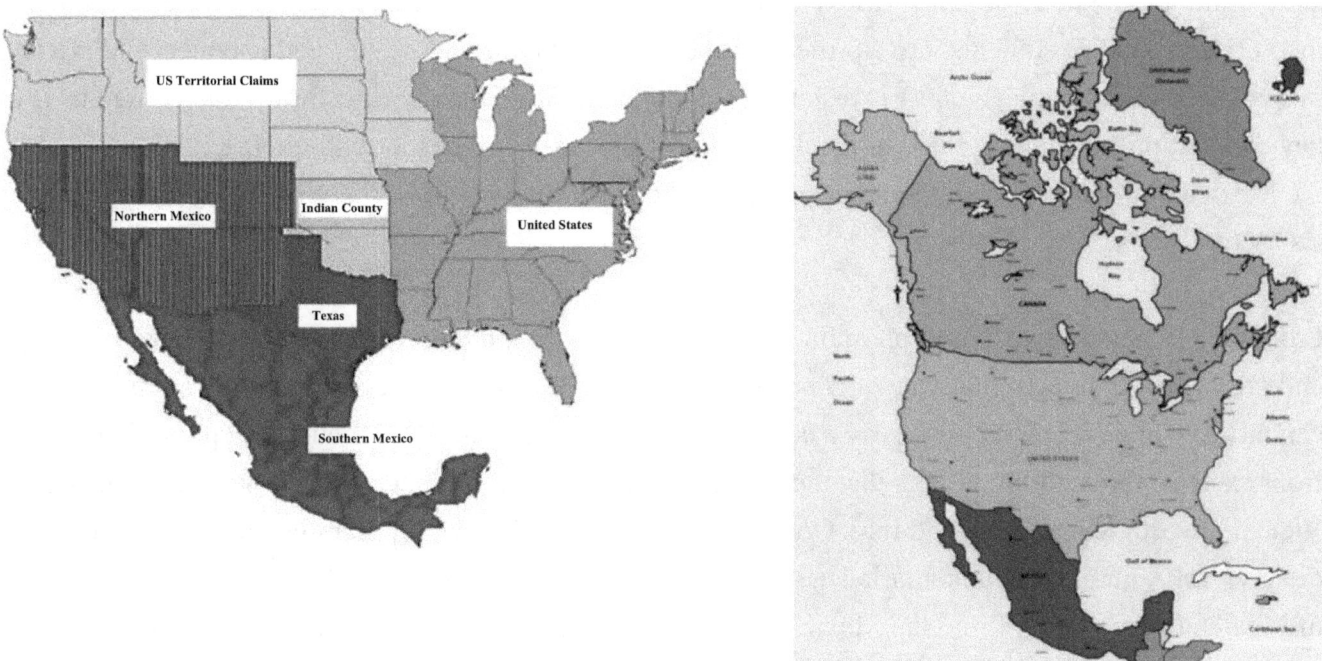

In contrast, the US Ambassador to Mexico, Carlos Pascual, resigned in March 2011, as a result, perhaps, of several years of bilateral tensions due to very active US/Mexican interaction in combating illegal drugs and organized crime. To understand how and why such cooperation and engagement could yield both positive and negative results, one must appreciate the complicated history and sensitivities between the two countries, especially involving the military. The following section briefly reviews the history underpinning Mexican military mistrust of their US defense counterparts.

Most US citizens do not realize that the average Mexican typically feels a deep sense of nationalistic indignation regarding past US violations of Mexico's sovereignty.[5] As Alan Riding once wrote, "Differences of history, religion, race and language serve to complicate... [and] widen the gulf of understanding that separates [Mexico and the United States]."[6] Within this context, for example, we in the United States do not consider the importance Mexicans place on events such as: Texas's declaration of independence from Mexico in 1836 and its accession to the United States in 1845; the US war with Mexico from 1846–48, which resulted in the annexation of Mexican territory, including what are now the states of California, Arizona, New Mexico, Nevada, Utah, and parts of Colorado and Wyoming; the US Naval occupation of Veracruz, Mexico, in 1914; and US punitive expeditions into Mexico in 1916 and 1917 to hunt for Pancho Villa after his raid into Columbus, New Mexico. Mexicans have been instructed since childhood that these historical events are an affront to their national pride. Even more intensely, the Mexican military has made this historical baggage a part of their professional

5 The title of Alan Riding's book on US-Mexico relations, *Distant Neighbors: A Portrait of the Mexicans* (New York: Vintage Books, 2000), captures the spirit of that sentiment.
6 Riding, pp. 16–317.

9

ethos. Accordingly, the concept of cooperating with members of the US armed forces was unpleasant at best and unthinkable for some.[7] Mexican military academies and other formal military educational institutions socialize students into a professional culture that embodies myths and legends of Mexican military heroes defending against invasions from the north. Vigilance against future US incursions is a key element of that culture. So, while polite and professional in demeanor with their US counterparts, the Mexican military has traditionally considered the US military its adversary in both a historical and a structural sense.

From the US perspective, Mexican military leaders work within an extraordinarily centralized system and are generally hypersensitive to any perceived slight. The United States has not viewed the Mexican military in hostile terms in nearly a century and has for many decades focused on preparing to confront external threats from potential competitors in faraway countries such as the Soviet Union, North Vietnam, North Korea, Iraq, and Iran. On the other hand, the Mexican military has focused on internal defense tasks, including humanitarian assistance and disaster relief, drug eradication, and the defense of Mexican sovereignty. From the Mexican perspective, US decision makers lack an understanding of and appreciation for Mexico's sovereignty-related concerns. Two examples may help to highlight these conflicting sensitivities, especially regarding organizational changes the United States has made to its system of commands that relate to Mexico.[8]

First, Mexico reacted heatedly in 2000 to a possible change to Mexico's status and organizational interface in dealing with a US Combatant Command, the US Southern Command (USSOUTHCOM). Until 2002, only three countries, Mexico, Canada, and Russia, had not been assigned within any Combatant Command "Area of Responsibility" (AOR). Based on this structure, senior Mexican military leaders dealt directly with their titular US defense establishment counterparts—the US Secretary of Defense, the Chairman of the Joint Chiefs of Staff, and Service Secretaries and Chiefs of Staff—even though their offices are not designed to accomplish the functional tasks that relate to defense relations with foreign countries. A senior US military official from the US Southern Command implied publicly that USSOUTHCOM might soon include Mexico in its AOR. In response, Mexican Foreign Minister Rosario Green voiced her outrage on the front page of Mexican newspapers, noting that "Mexico would not accept coming under the responsibility of USSOUTHCOM."[9] To reduce the tension, the United States immediately invited then Mexican Secretary of Defense General Enrique Cervantes Aguirre to visit

---

7 Deare, p. 2.

8 There are some important organizational differences between US and Mexican military structures. The US has a civilian Secretary of Defense and civilian defense infrastructure that manages and provides oversight of US defense forces; whereas Mexico has two separate ministries under the control of two military officers who direct the armed forces. The Mexican Secretary of National Defense is traditionally an Army Four Star General who commands and controls the Army and the Air Force. The Secretary of the Navy is a four star navy admiral, who controls the Navy and Marine Corps. The concept of civilian leadership of the Mexican military—by any official under the President—has been debated, but is not expected to occur in the near future.

9 Elena Medina, "Defienden soberanía en lucha contra el narco," *Reforma*, January 6, 2000, Mexico City, Mexico, p. 1. The actual quote is: "El Gobierno no acepta la incorporación de México al Comando Sur de Estados Unidos, afirmó ayer Rosario Green, Secretaria de Relaciones Exteriores quien agregó que no se acepta nada que pueda vulnerar la soberanía."

10

July 2011 Volume 1 Number 1
Strategic Issues in U.S.-Latin American Relations
Critical Strategic Decisions in Mexico: the Future of US/Mexican Defense Relations

then US Secretary of Defense William Cohen, Chairman of the Joint Chiefs of Staff General Hugh Shelton, Secretary of the Army Luis Caldera, and Army Chief of Staff General Eric Shinseki. All these office calls took place in one day, which was the length of time General Cervantes said he was willing to spend in the United States.[10] During that visit, General Shelton took pains to assure General Cervantes that the United States would not place Mexico within the AOR of a Combatant Command—at least "during my watch" (meaning during his time as Chairman of the Joint Chiefs of Staff). In essence, Mexico viewed any change to direct lines of coordination with the US Secretary of Defense and Chairman of the Joint Chiefs as evidence of US intent to snub Mexico.[11] Moreover, given their national doctrine of "nonintervention," Mexico interpreted any effort to associate Mexico with a "Combatant" Command to be highly offensive. In the end, following significant damage control, the United States took Mexican concerns into account.

In the second case, Mexican leaders again took offense when the United States actually did place Mexico within the AOR for a newly created combatant command, the US Northern Command (USNORTHCOM). As a consequence of the tragic events of September 11, 2001, the United States reorganized its national security organizational structure to create the US Northern Command[12] and assigned it with missions including homeland defense, defense support of civilian authorities, and, later, security cooperation with Mexico, Canada, and the Bahamas. The Mexican media criticized this organizational restructuring, and the Mexican military leadership highlighted their objections to any change from working directly through the OSD, the Joint Staff, and the Services. SEDENA's Deputy Chief of Operations declared that Mexico had absolutely nothing to do with the US Northern Command.[13] Then Secretary of National Defense Gen. Ricardo Clemente Vega Garcia also testified in the Mexican Congress that the Mexican Army and Air Force would not participate in USNORTHCOM operations or programs.[14] At this point, the stage was set for poor Mexican cooperation with USNORTHCOM.[15]

---

10 Reportedly, General Cervantes said that since the US Army Chief of Staff's previous visit to Mexico had been for only one day, his visit as the Mexican Secretary of Defense would only be one day in the US.
11 Mexico has no equivalent to a Joint Staff. In the US system, geographic "Combatant Commands," such as the US Southern Command or the US European Command, handle functional coordination and security cooperation issues for foreign countries.
12 Along with the Department of Homeland Security.
13 Graham H. Turbiville, "US Military Engagement with Mexico: An Easy Past and Challenging Future," Joint Special Operations University Report 10-2, March 2010, p. 28.
14 Turbiville, pg. 28.
15 In recent years, relations with SEMAR have been much more cordial and practical in an operational sense than with the Secretariat of National Defense, which have typically been formal, if not prickly, at best. Because of its key role in the Mexican Revolution, the Mexican Army has traditionally been seen as a guardian of the Mexican revolutionary state. In contrast, as former Secretary of the Mexican Navy Admiral Lorenzo Franco once told me, "Borders separate us, but the ocean [on which there are no clear-cut borders] unifies us."

11

July 2011 Volume 1 Number 1
Strategic Issues in U.S.-Latin American Relations
Critical Strategic Decisions in Mexico: the Future of US/Mexican Defense Relations

The Catalyst for Improved US/Mexican Defense Relations: President Calderón's Decision to Confront Transnational Criminal Organizations

Considering this background, the level of positive interaction between the United States and Mexican militaries since the Calderón administration took office has been remarkable. In a recent article, former USNORTHCOM Commander General Gene Renuart and Dr. Biff Baker highlight that analysts—especially those who have known US/Mexican relations over past decades—do not realize how rapidly US/Mexican military-to-military relations have advanced over the last three years.[16] Why and how did the US/Mexico defense relationship change so quickly to a point at which the past and current USNORTHCOM commanders would state publicly that this relationship has, in such a short time, become better than at any time in our history?[17]

Upon assuming office in 2006, Mexican President Felipe Calderón made several courageous decisions that helped set the foundation for the currently positive US/Mexico defense relationship.[18] His decision to use the military to combat TCOs was the catalyst that helped change the US/Mexico defense relationship dramatically. Calderón assessed that the police lacked professionalism and were too corrupt to fight the narcotraffickers, so he decided that the Mexican military was the only option to lead the fight against drug-related violence and associated criminal activity. He also published a national strategy directing greater cooperation with Mexico's neighbors (meaning the United States) on matters of mutual interest. The Mexican military neither asked for nor wanted this nontraditional mission, having little experience in the activities that entailed direct, daily confrontation with organized crime. The very nature of military operations to attack and destroy enemy objectives is contrary to the type of activities required in police work, which includes interacting consistently within the community, investigating crimes, and protecting evidence. While the military had previously been called upon to provide personnel to previous law enforcement initiatives such as the Federal Preventive Police under the control of the Office of the Attorney General, this mission was tangential for the military. Moreover, involvement in these violent urban areas led to charges of human rights violations against the Mexican military. This lack of preparation for a nontraditional policing mission in an urban environment, coupled with the President's mandate to work with the United States, gradually pushed the Mexican military to work more closely with the United States. In sum, President Calderón's tasking of his military to confront

---

16 Renuart and Baker, pp. 1, 4.

17 Adm. James Winnefeld, comments (with permission), San Miguel de Allende, Mexico, October 2010.

18 Although President Calderón's decision to use the Mexican military to confront the TCOs is a courageous political act from any perspective, some critics believe otherwise. Rather than a courageous decision to confront the rampant corruption and growing power and influence of the drug trafficking organizations, their perspective holds that President Calderón's decision was made for purely political reasons. In a very close presidential election in 2006, President Calderón had won over his PRD opponent, Andres Manuel Lopez Obrador, by a margin of less than one percentage point. Lopez Obrador refused to concede the victory and declared himself the "Legitimate President." He and his supporters then camped out for months in the Main Plaza in Mexico City. This perspective asserts that President Calderón deployed the military to demonstrate that, as the President and Commander in Chief, it was he rather than Lopez Obrador who had the legitimacy to control the military forces. However, regardless of the motivation, his decision to take on the TCOs placed him and his family at great personal danger. His decision has also made a dramatic and important statement concerning the need for Mexico to eliminate impunity and bring about the rule of law that should characterize life in a true democracy.

12

the TCOs in coordination with the United States placed both the Mexican and US militaries in a position to focus on a common threat on both sides of the border—for the first time in many years.

Navy Admiral Mike Mullen, Chairman of the Joint Chiefs of Staff, talks to a former 201st Fighter Squadron member at Chapultepec Park in Mexico City, March 6, 2009.

The "Mérida Initiative" was another critical point in US/Mexican efforts to confront drug violence and arms trafficking perpetrated by organized crime. Presidents Calderón and Bush agreed upon this program in the city of Mérida, Mexico, in October 2007. To facilitate Department of Defense (DOD) support for the Mérida Initiative, US Secretary of Defense Robert Gates visited Mexico in April 2008 (the second such visit by a US Secretary of Defense).[19] In meetings with Mexican officials Gates emphasized that the DOD would help train and develop educational and informational exchanges for Mexican forces in a manner deferential to Mexican sovereignty.[20] Subsequently, the Mexican military gradually became willing to accept US assistance, equipment, training, information, and intelligence exchanges, as well as a variety of programs regarding strategic and operational leadership and campaign planning.

Visits by other US and Mexican senior defense officials were pivotal in this process. The chairman of the Joint Chiefs of Staff, Admiral Michael Mullen, visited Mexico in March 2009 and met with both Secretary of National Defense General Guillermo Galván Galván and Secretary of the Navy Admiral Mariano Francisco Saynéz. Shortly thereafter, the Mexican Senate approved participation by the Mexican Navy in the April to May 2009 multinational UNITAS exercise. USNORTHCOM, initially in conjunction with the Center for Hemispheric Defense Studies, began hosting a series of visits by senior Mexican naval, governmental, and political leaders to USNORTHCOM in Colorado Springs, Colorado.

The Mexican Secretariat of National Defense (SEDENA—the Army and Air Force under the Secretary of National Defense) declined to send Army or Air Force officers to USNORTHCOM in those first visits. However, over time, USNORTHCOM began to host conferences on themes such as pandemic influenza and cooperation on Mexico's southern border with Guatemala and Belize, events in which SEDENA representatives began to participate. In a symbolically important visit in September 2007, then USNORTHCOM Commander General Gene Renuart traveled to Mexico to meet with Admiral

---

19 Secretary William Perry made the first-ever visit of a serving US Secretary of Defense to Mexico in 1995.
20 Turbiville, pp. 31-32. Gates stressed that no US combat troops would be involved and that Mexico would determine the requirements.

13

Francisco Saynéz Mendoza and General Guillermo Galván Galván during "El Grito," the annual celebration of Mexico's struggle for independence from Spain. Even more significantly, these top Mexican Navy and Army officials made visits to USNORTHCOM in 2008 and 2009.

General Douglas Fraser, Commander, USSOUTHCOM; Admiral Mariano Francisco Saynez Mendoza, Mexican Secretary of the Navy; and Admiral James Winnefeld (at the time of this photograph), Commander, USNORTHCOM.

As concrete examples of increasingly close cooperation, the Mexican Navy Secretariat (SEMAR) established a liaison officer position at USNORTHCOM in 2007, and SEDENA established a liaison officer position at USNORTHCOM in 2009. After taking command of USNORTHCOM in May 2010, Admiral James Winnefeld continued to deepen military-to-military relations with Mexico. He placed a high priority on engagement with Mexico and conducted several personal visits with his Mexican counterparts, General Galván and Admiral Saynéz in both the United States and Mexico. He also ensured that key members of his staff traveled frequently to Mexico to work closely with the Mexican military on a wide range of information-sharing, intelligence, and campaign-planning–related programs. For example, Major General Larry Stutzriem, NORTHCOM's Director of Plans, Policy and Strategy, made 14 official visits to Mexico during his tenure from June 2009 to July 2011. Combined with NORTHCOM's hosting of many Mexican delegations in the United States, these activities constituted an unprecedented level of interaction.[21]

Equipment transfers made possible through the Mérida Initiative were also important because they helped validate the credibility of the US commitment to assisting Mexican military forces. US-

21 Discussions with Maj. Gen. Larry Stutzriem, NORTHCOM's Director of Plans, Policy and Strategy, and other NORTHCOM staff officials, January–May, 2011.

14

July 2011 Volume 1 Number 1
Strategic Issues in U.S.-Latin American Relations
Critical Strategic Decisions in Mexico: the Future of US/Mexican Defense Relations

NORTHCOM coordinated the delivery of aircraft and helicopters, night vision goggles, rigid hull inflatable boats, and protective ensembles, as well as tactical communications equipment intended to improve the Mexican military's ability to deploy rapid reaction forces in support of police operations against drug cartels and to help conduct maritime surveillance.[22] Additionally, USNORTHCOM facilitated pilot training and information exchanges designed to help develop specialized capabilities to share intelligence information, thereby enhancing Mexican security force operations' ability to systematically dismantle the TCOs.

A Maturing, But Still Fragile US/Mexico Defense Relationship

Can and will this positive engagement last? As noted above, the extent to which the US/Mexican defense relationship has advanced in the past few years is significant and surprising. However, the public revelation of diplomatic documents in late 2010 caused damage to the environment. In such documents, US officials purportedly criticized Mexican efforts and ability to combat organized crime. Reportedly, Mexican officials, including President Calderón, were angered by comments questioning the Mexican Army's reluctance to act on information the United States had provided about drug trafficker Arturo Beltrán Leyva (later killed in an assault by Mexican Marines acting on the same information) Calderón.[23] The question is whether relations will continue to strengthen and improve, or return to their traditional formal and distant state. Additionally, will institutional or political factors be more important in determining future US/Mexican defense relations?

One school of thought, expressed in 2010 by a number of currently serving US and Mexican military officers, posits that the current US/Mexican defense relationship can never return to its traditional state, especially given the range of economic, diplomatic, and military issues that keep our nations intertwined.[24] The present state of political tensions between Mexico and the United States has tempered this optimistic viewpoint, however. During an official visit to Washington D.C. in early March 2011 to meet with his US counterpart, President Calderón publicly criticized US Ambassador to Mexico Carlos Pascual. Ambassador Pascual's subsequent resignation was in large part merely a public manifestation of these tensions.[25] More to the point for the purpose of this paper, political concerns caused an impact in defense and military relations. Reportedly, these tensions had a chilling effect on US relations with the Mexican Army and Air Force.

22 Statement by General Victor E. Renaurt Jr., USAF, Commander United States Northern Command and North American Aerospace Defense Command beore the Senate Armed Services Committee 11 March 2010, pp. 24-25. http://armed-services.senate.gov/statemnt/2010/03%20March/Renuart%2003-11-10.pdf.
23 Damien Cave and Ginger Thompson, "After US Envoy Quits in Mexico, Questions Arise on Cooperation in Drug War," in *The New York Times*, March 26, 2011, p. A-10. "US Ambassador Resigns amid Uproar over Leaked Cable," *Latin America Advisor*, Inter-American Dialogue, March 21, 2011, p. 3.
24 Interviews with US officials at USNORTHCOM and Mexican Army and Navy officers, February–May, 2010.
25 Damien Cave, "Envoy Quits over Cable's on Mexico," *New York Times*, March 20, March 2011, http://www.nytimes.com/2011/03/20/world/americas/20mexico.html?-r1&sq=carlospascual.

15

July 2011 Volume 1 Number 1
Strategic Issues in U.S.-Latin American Relations
Critical Strategic Decisions in Mexico: the Future of US/Mexican Defense Relations

US NORTHCOM coordinated with the Mexican Army and Air Force to load a Mexican Army field kitchen on board a US Air Force C-5 bound for Haiti, February 6, 2010.

Another school of thought, expressed by National Defense University Professor Craig Deare, holds that Mexico is capable of short-term alliances when it perceives a threat to its security and its interests; however, relations will revert to their historically distant status after those periods of positive relations.[26] For example, during World War II, the two countries formed the Joint Mexican–United States Defense Commission (JMUSDC), and Mexico sent the famous Mexican Fighter Squadron 201, the "Aztec Eagles," to fly close air support missions for US troops in the Philippines. Yet, following the war, a languishing JMUSDC became a symbol of Mexico's unwillingness to cooperate further with the United States. Another important period of cooperation followed then Secretary of Defense William Perry's landmark visit to Mexico in 1995. As a consequence of their personal warmth and interaction, Secretary Perry and his Mexican counterpart, Gen. Enrique Cervantes Aguirre, established a US/ Mexico Bilateral Working Group that markedly helped advance the US/Mexico defense relationship. Gradually, it returned to its normal, "distant," level after Secretary Perry left the Pentagon in 1997. US acceptance of Mexico's offer to provide assistance in the aftermath of Hurricane Katrina in 2005 also helped create a temporary period of good will between the two militaries.

26 Deare, p. 3.

16

July 2011 Volume 1 Number 1
Strategic Issues in U.S.-Latin American Relations
Critical Strategic Decisions in Mexico: the Future of US/Mexican Defense Relations

Which perspective appears more feasible? It is still too early to be sure how this situation will develop. Nevertheless, Mexico's strategic decisions as well as US policies will affect this relationship in a dynamic way. As noted above, recent political events appear to buttress this second school of thought and cast a dark shadow on the perspective that institutional factors will determine the future trajectory of the US/Mexico defense relationship. Even during this period of extraordinary US/Mexican defense and military cooperation, the issue of meaningful coordination in operational activities has been very sensitive. The Mexican government was not anxious to facilitate the establishment of combined operations involving US and Mexican military organizations in Mexico—or even to admit that US personnel had been involved in activities in Mexico.

3. Where is the Relationship Going—and Why?
Potential Options for Critical Strategic Decision

Considering the foregoing discussion, the most potentially significant determinant regarding the future of US/Mexican defense relations involves a decision by the next president of Mexico, either to maintain or to change Mexico's current approach to confronting TCOs. This section seeks to offer insight regarding how future political decisions to be made by the next president of Mexico will lead to different possible future paths for US/Mexican defense relations. Based on his speech in the United States in June 2010 and his consistent responses to challenging security situations, President Calderón apparently intends to maintain a hard line against the drug cartels through the end of his "sexenio (six-year term)."[27] The next presidential election in Mexico is scheduled for July 2012 and President Calderón's successor will take office in December 2012. Politics in Mexico are volatile and electoral campaign scenarios can change rapidly. Nevertheless, projections from the results of recent mid-term congressional elections and governors' races lead most analysts (at the time of this writing) to predict that the PRI is likely to win the presidential election in 2012.[28] The question of presidential succession is certainly relevant and influences the analysis in the foregoing sections. That said, it is not necessary to accurately predict the outcome of those elections to evaluate the options that any incoming government would and must consider.

Once elected, be it a PAN, PRI, or PRD government,[29] the new administration will use the presidential transition as an opportunity to assess its options and determine how best to achieve a variety of domestic and foreign policy objectives for the six years ahead. Indeed, the public's perception and level

---

27 Joint Statement from President Barack Obama and President Felipe Calderón, May 19, 2010. http://www.cfr.org/mexico/joint-statement-president-barack-obama-president-felipe-caldern-may-2010/p22518. Remarks by President Obama and President Calderón of Mexico at the Joint Press Availability, May 19, 2010. http://www.whitehouse.gov/the-press-office/remarks-president-obama-and-president-calder-n-mexico-joint-press-availability.

28 Politics in Mexico are enormously vibrant and rapidly changeable, but the state-of-play of presidential politics at the time of this writing would indicate a distinct advantage for the PRI in the next election. Conflicts among fractions within the PRD make a victory by a PRD candidate appear less likely. The PAN has yet to field a popular candidate.

29 The main political parties in Mexico are: the Institutional Revolutionary Party (PRI), which held power for 70 years until 2000; the centrist National Action Party (PAN), which has held office since 2000; and the leftist Democratic Revolutionary Party (PRD).

17

of popular support for the current strategy will be important factors. A PRI or a PRD administration would be more likely to label Calderón's PAN administration strategy a complete failure and would be likely to choose a distinctly different approach.[30] Yet, even a PAN president would seek to differentiate his or her policies and show independence from President Calderón.[31]

Rather than attempt to predict the future, this article takes the perspective that the new presidential administration in Mexico will consider whether to continue the Calderón administration's approach of confronting TCOs or to initiate an alternative strategy. This section offers four strategic options that represent the range of scenarios available to the next president of Mexico; it also analyzes the potential consequences each option portends for the structure of the US/Mexico defense relationship. The first option is essentially to stay the course with the current Calderón administration's approach. The second option would modify the current strategy to place the locus of effort squarely on law-enforcement and eliminate or dramatically reduce the use of military forces in the war against the TCOs. The third option represents a variety of possibilities that maintain a sincere effort to confront organized crime, but reflect socially focused alternatives to a confrontational or repressive strategy against the TCOs. The fourth option highlights a choice to turn back to the corporatist PRI's old ways of doing business, by either tacitly or openly seeking accommodation with the cartels. The following sections present each of these options in turn, along with a discussion of the potential impact each option would have in terms of institutionalizing US/Mexico defense relations.

Option A. Continue the Calderón Administration's Strategy against TCOs and Impunity (Military Lead Role)

1). Discussion of option.

This "stay the course" option presumes that the next president of Mexico, regardless of party, would continue the drug war with the same focus and intensity as would the Calderón administration. The rationale underpinning such a decision posits that the next administration asserts Mexico must exercise real sovereignty and rule of law over its territory in order to be a viable, effective democracy. This option implicitly presumes that there is no turning back from Mexico's current level of effort in combating the impunity that illegal organizations now enjoy. Additionally, this option encompasses the

---

30 From a political perspective, Option A, "the stay the course" option, would not be the most likely course of action for a PRI administration. In a question-and-answer session following his speech at the Woodrow Wilson Center in Washington, D.C., in 2010, the leading PRI candidate, Gov. Enrique Pena Nieto commented that placing the responsibility for confronting organized crime on the police and reducing the military's role in that effort was a distinct possibility. Nonetheless, once a government is in office, a measure of pragmatism often tempers campaign rhetoric.

31 As we have seen in the US, when a new president from the same party takes office there may be a structural sense of continuity, but the new administration will appoint new personnel to key positions and will try to distinguish its policies from its predecessor. For example, when Republican President George Herbert Walker Bush followed Republican President Ronald Reagan, many were surprised at the numbers of changes in political appointees, as well as some differences in approach. We may expect a greater degree of continuity with an incoming PAN administration and a greater likelihood of change in policy with a PRI administration.

18

July 2011 Volume 1 Number 1
Strategic Issues in U.S.-Latin American Relations
Critical Strategic Decisions in Mexico: the Future of US/Mexican Defense Relations

concept that the United States and Mexico are integrally linked in this fight; hence, a coordinated international effort is necessary to address criminal organizations on both sides of the border through the Mérida Initiative or a similar approach that will provide better results. Finally, this option assumes that the administration would continue to use the Mexican military in a direct role to confront the TCOs until police reform programs now under way permit the police to take the lead role, which could take years to accomplish.

US Army forces training Mexican Marines, December 4, 2010; Agence France-Presse.

The Calderón administration's fight against the TCOs has been difficult. In response to his administration's direct attack on corruption, the violence in Mexico dramatically increased to nearly 6,000 narcotics-related deaths per year since 2007 and more than 10,000 in 2010.[32] The violence has taken place primarily in border zones and drug trafficking corridors leading to the US market, called "plazas." Ninety percent of drug-related deaths have involved conflicts between the narcotraffickers themselves; about 6 percent represent deaths resulting from public security force conflicts with the cartels. The violence has begun to affect innocent people not related to the drug trafficking business, however. Surveys indicate that the popularity of Calderón's hard line approach toward confronting the TCOs has slipped. A poll published in February 2010 indicated that 50 percent of respondents believe the country is "less safe" because of government strategies; 47 percent of those polled think the current level of insecurity in Mexico is a sign of the failure of the Calderón administration's approach.[33] Moreover, Mexico perceives a lack of US commitment to the principle of shared responsibility, due to the slow delivery of equipment promised through the Mérida Initiative.[34] Some analysts have harshly criticized Calderón's approach in combating organized crime, and recommend dramatic changes in strategy. For example, two well-known observers

32 "Felipe Calderón," "Times Topics," *New York Times International Tribune* (global edition), April, 16, 2011; http://topics.nytimes.com/top/reference/timestopics/people/c/felipe_Calderón/index.html; Jacobo García, "México, 10.000 muertos, 33 día, 1.3 horas," *El Mundo*, November, 6, 2010. Newspapers statistics indicate that more than 34,000 violent deaths have occurred since the government of President Felipe Calderón took office (December 2006). Statistics offered in news articles such as these highlight the number of victims in Mexico each year related to the fight against organized crime to be approximately 2,275 in 2007; 5,207 in 2008; 6,587 in 2009; and more than 10,000 in 2010.

33 Survey regarding presidencial approval rating for President Felipe Calderón in Mexico, Buendía y Laredo, "Encuesta Nacional: Seguridad y Narcotráfico," February 2010, pp. 7, 11, 13.

34 Roger F. Noriega., "The Drug Fight in Mexico: Failure Is Not an Option," American Enterprise Institute for Public Policy Research, May 2010. http://www.aei.org/outlook/100957. Roger Noriega, "Latin American Action Agenda for the New Congress," American Enterprise Institute for Public Policy Research, January 2011, http://www.aei.org/outlook/101014. Jackson Diehl, "U.S. Falls Short in Helping Mexico End Its Drug War," *Washington Post*, January 26, 2010; http://www.washingtonpost.com/wp-dyn/content/article/2010/07/25/AR2010072502762.html.

19

July 2011 Volume 1 Number 1
Strategic Issues in U.S.-Latin American Relations
Critical Strategic Decisions in Mexico: the Future of US/Mexican Defense Relations

and former Mexican officials, Jorge Castañeda and Rubén Aguilar, have highlighted that the drug war is a US problem, not a Mexican issue; they propose ending repression against the TCOs in favor of an approach that reflects accommodation with the narcotraffickers.[35]

2). Impact on US/Mexico Defense Relationship.

The "stay the course" option would potentially offer an additional "sexenio" during which the US and Mexican militaries could expand and mature in the conduct of shared missions. If so, the growing relationship could potentially lead to a network or infrastructure of activities and agreements. Military forces from both countries would continue to exchange intelligence and sensitive information and share operational experiences while working toward a common purpose and objectives. Perhaps eventually, the United States and Mexico could engage in exercises as well as combined operations that would permit the development of tactics, techniques, and procedures that align their efforts not only in the fight against the TCOs, but also in other functional areas such as disaster or humanitarian relief operations, cooperative responses to terrorism, or proliferation of WMDs. Beyond mere confidence-building measures, this process could ideally lead to the establishment of protocols or standard operating procedures through which the forces of the two countries could operate in a common framework and ultimately achieve a level of functional interoperability.

Although the US/Mexican defense relationship has advanced significantly in the past few years—certainly more quickly than any analyst would have predicted—the relationship is still not mature, stable, or consolidated. The strong US/Canada defense relationship offers a useful example of how military-to-military relations can mitigate the long-term impact of political decisions made on the basis of short-term disagreements between nations. The defense relationship with Canada, for example, involves a rich tradition of agreements and joint commissions, including a bi-national command, such as the US/Canada Permanent Joint Board on Defense, established in 1948; the Military Cooperation Committee (MCC), since 1945; and the North America Aerospace Defense Command, based in Colorado Springs, Colorado, which is literally a two-nation command. While cooperative US/Mexican military-to-military initiatives seem to increase almost monthly, there is a long way to go before the United States and Mexico can achieve the kind of mature defense partnership that characterizes the US/Canada relationship. The US/Mexico defense relationship is not yet at a point in which institutional factors can help mitigate political tensions between the two countries.

Time is the key element in advancing toward a more institutionalized structure of bilateral or even trilateral cooperation. At a minimum, a sustained process is needed for the US and Mexican militaries to continually enhance their relationship in a manner that benefits both countries. Continuing on the present course would probably entail more and more intrusive U.S. cooperation, both for equipment and

---

35 Rubén Aguilar V. and Jorge Castañeda, *El Narco: La Guerra Fallida* (Mexico City: Punto de Lectura, 2009).

training of Mexican law enforcement personnel, as well as for intelligence and other tactical support.

The lofty, ultimate goal of such a process from a US viewpoint could be the establishment of a bi-national or even tri-national command in Mexico, addressing humanitarian assistance and disaster relief, as well as protection of critical infrastructure intelligence sharing, cyber security, counterterrorism, and perhaps support for counter-TCO efforts. Ideally, this multinational security organization could be under the leadership of a Mexican military or civilian official.[36] While international military organizations such as NATO or even NORAD could serve as models, even in the most optimistic of scenarios that level of US/Mexican, and potentially Canadian, cooperation would require many years—even decades—of sustained effort and interaction. As increasing numbers of Mexican military personnel work closely with their US counterparts for longer periods of time, there could be a corresponding reduction in the stigma and barriers to a closer US/Mexico defense relationship arising from our past history.

If the next administration retains the current approach of emphasizing military involvement in the effort in confronting the TCOs, the outlook toward sustained enhancement in the US/Mexican defense relationship would be very positive. Ongoing US/Mexican programs would presumably continue and expand. Accordingly, this option keeps the US and Mexican defense establishments focused on the same mission: facilitating integrated national and international efforts to combat the TCOs, a common enemy.[37] Institutional arrangements would continue and personal and professional relationships would be strengthened. In short, Option A would facilitate a continued process of greater understanding and increased interoperability between the two militaries. Conceivably, over time US and Mexican defense and military organizations would be working in coordinated or even integrated arrangements.

---

36 Such a scenario seems radical today. However, it is worth noting that the establishment of the North American Aerospace Defense Command (NORAD) in 1957 was also controversial. The development of NORAD's unique command and control procedures, which now seem routine, was a response to those original concerns. Can we not envision a future situation in which the US and Mexico or even the US, Mexico, and Canada form a combined command to address common challenges? Some analysts have advocated the incorporation of Mexico into the North American Aerospace Defense Command, currently a bi-national US/Canada command. See James Carafano, Jena Baker McNeill, Ray Walser, Richard Weitz, "Expand NORAD to Improve Security in North America," Heritage Foundation Backgrounder, July 27, 2010, Washington, D.C; http://www.heritage.org/Research/Reports/2010/07/Expand-NORAD-to-Improve-Security-in-North-America. That approach would be particularly sensitive for Mexico, as it would place Mexico in a subordinate position to the US. A bi-national US/Mexico command, or even a tri-national US/Canada/Mexico command in Mexico, under the command of a Mexican military official, may be a more feasible approach.

37 Without such a shared objective, the Mexican military could return to their traditional missions, one of which would be defending against an attack from the US.

21

Option B. Assign Law Enforcement (Rather than the Military) the Lead Role in Combating TCOs.

1). Discussion of Option.

Convoys of Mexican law enforcement and security forces during a major urban training exercise.

The next presidential administration in Mexico could also opt to confront organized crime by placing the locus of effort on law enforcement rather than the military. Such an approach would afford the next president of Mexico several advantages. First, it offers the political value of a fresh start for a Mexican public weary of years of violence and conflict. The incoming administration could coin a new label for its strategy, distinguishing its new approach from the Mérida Initiative. Along that line, that shift would showcase a marked difference from the Calderón administration, highlighting its response to the declining popularity of the military-led offensive on the TCOs. Second, the new strategy would allow the president to place the responsibility for confronting organized crime on the police, which from a structural perspective is the appropriate institution. Third, a police-led effort would in fact be popular with the Mexican military. The Army in particular does not view urban police operations as an appropriate mission and has been charged with many human rights violations resulting from its involvement in urban areas. Finally, within an international context, this approach would continue to demonstrate US and Mexican cooperation in the fight against drugs and organized crime.

The long-term solution to Mexico's fight against the TCOs must ultimately involve an effective, competent, and honest police force. Both President Vicente Fox (2000–2006) and his successor, President

22

July 2011 Volume 1 Number 1
Strategic Issues in U.S.-Latin American Relations
Critical Strategic Decisions in Mexico: the Future of US/Mexican Defense Relations

Calderón intended to establish more competent, better-trained police forces that could more effectively combat the TCOs.[38] Indeed, the Calderón administration views the use of the military as a necessary, but not permanent, long-term solution to the problem of drug violence in Mexico. President Calderón pushed to increase the size and capability of the federal police force and to reorganize the highly corruptible (and often corrupted) 2,021 municipal police forces into 32 state-level police forces. The intended result was to be better, more standardized training and increased pay to make the police less susceptible to bribes, as well as greater accountability and oversight. To that end, during his administration the federal police force has been increased from 6,000 officers to 35,000 officers from 2008 until 2011, although the bill to create and reconstitute the state-level police forces has not yet been passed. Nevertheless, such actions could not be an effective solution during President Calderón's term in office.

The police reforms required to achieve the nationwide police coordination necessary to address organized crime and maintain the rule of law will take years to accomplish. The task of reforming the police to build capacity, professionalize, and reduce corruption to a point at which the police could take the lead against the TCOs is a particularly daunting challenge in Mexico. This task involves the enactment of significant legislation (always a difficult proposition in Mexico), as well as the recruitment, training and structural reforms, and reorganization of the police in ways needed to meet security requirements. While police forces reform and reorganize to assume the lead role, heavy military involvement in the effort to confront organized crime in Mexico would likely continue throughout much if not the entirety of the next president's term.

2). Impact on US/Mexico Defense Relationship.

The selection of Option B would not sustain or advance US and Mexican defense and military relations as far as under Option A. However, this option would potentially facilitate conditions for positive improvements to the defense relationship. The significant difference from Option A involves the duration of direct US/Mexican military-to-military cooperation in the counter TCO effort. US/Mexican defense and military contacts will reduce accordingly during the transition to a police lead role. In that period, the Mexican military would presumably continue to support the police, which could potentially offer useful opportunities for sustained US/Mexican defense and military collaboration and cooperation in key functional areas. Moreover, even after the police eventually take the lead role in combating the TCOs, the military will most likely still be required to assist the police force with intelligence and the planning of intelligence-driven operations, as well as logistical and occasional operational support, which provides further opportunities for US/Mexican defense collaboration.

---

38 President Vicente Fox worked hard to provide the Federal Preventative Police with the necessary resources and technology to continue fighting drug cartels. "El Presidente Fox entregó equipamiento a la Policía Federal Preventiva," April 4, 2002. http://fox .presidencia.gob mx/actividades/?contenido=2829.

23

July 2011 Volume 1 Number 1
Strategic Issues in U.S.-Latin American Relations
Critical Strategic Decisions in Mexico: the Future of US/Mexican Defense Relations

Under Option B, the military would retain a lead role in combating organized crime for perhaps four or more years during the next administration to allow for the transition to a police lead. During that time, it is probable that US/Mexican defense and military interaction and cooperation programs will also continue to strengthen. The same kinds of information, intelligence, training, and operational exchanges and support that are occurring now should continue. Accordingly, US and Mexican defense and military organizations will have worked cooperatively with increasingly closer ties for the six years of the Calderón administration and perhaps four or more years during the next administration. Such sustained interaction is likely to help deepen ties between defense and military personnel from the two countries, allowing the stigma and institutional resistance of working with their US counterparts to diminish.

Once the Mexican police take the lead role in combating organized crime, combined US/Mexican defense interactions may begin to decrease. The relationship could still continue to be positive, although not as intense as at current levels. In all likelihood, the Mexican military would continue to support the police, rather than mounting separate operations against the TCOs. Under this scenario, the military would not patrol the streets, but may be expected to mount occasional raid-type operations when intelligence indicates the possibility of capturing highly armed and entrenched kingpins, or to seize heavily protected strongholds where drugs or weapons are cached. The military may also be involved in strike operations when information must be closely guarded; when the expected TCO response may exceed the police's capability; or when a military-type operation would be more appropriate.

Operations involving the police, the military, and other local, state, and federal entities are difficult to coordinate; accordingly, the United States may continue to be able to offer useful assistance. The US military has significant experience in operating in integrated, inter-institutional efforts in domestic as well as foreign operations, as in Iraq and Afghanistan. While acting in a support, rather than a lead role, US forces often help to coordinate the efforts of federal, state, and local agencies, or at least provide a secure venue in which to conduct planning and coordination activities. The Mexican military is already operating in support of the police in this manner in some parts of the country. In one successful example, known as the "Tijuana Model," in the state of the Baja California the former Army Zone Commander helped coordinate the efforts of the police, military, and other federal and state entities. He also provided a protected location on the Army base from which to plan, coordinate, prepare, and initiate deployment of operations against the TCOs operating in that zone.[39] This supporting role is critical, as military forces tend to have significant resources and the ability to facilitate coordination among disparate agencies. Nevertheless, this model is not consistently applied in different zones in Mexico.

Given the difficulty of this type of action requiring "interagency coordination," the United States could conceivably offer and share useful experience, tactics, techniques, and procedures with their Mexican

---

39 Eric. L. Olson, David A. Shirk, and Andrew Selee, editors, "Shared Responsibility: U.S.-Mexico Policy Options for Confronting Organized Crime," Woodrow Wilson International Center for Scholars, October 2010.

24

July 2011 Volume 1 Number 1
Strategic Issues in U.S.-Latin American Relations
Critical Strategic Decisions in Mexico: the Future of US/Mexican Defense Relations

counterparts. In the past several years, the Mexican military has been receptive to US experience, assistance, and advice because of their need to conduct the difficult mission of confronting the TCOs—a task with which they had little experience. US military forces have significant experience in nontraditional operations and have coordinated actions in ways analogous to the "Tijuana Model."

Option C. Adopt a New Violence-Reduction Strategy Addressesing the Social Causes Underpinning Mexico's Culture of Lawlessness and Impunity

1). Discussion of Option.

This option envisions a strategy by which the next presidential administration in Mexico could attempt to reduce violence through socially based or "non-repressive" programs. These programs fall within a range of openly discussed, but relatively novel, alternatives purporting to address the social causes that facilitate and exacerbate the rise of organized crime and drug trafficking and the violence they generate. Rather than a confrontational approach that seeks to disrupt or dismantle the TCOs, this option encompasses social approaches designed to foster a "culture of lawfulness" in Mexico that could include policy changes such as decriminalization or legalization.

As an example of a socially based alternative, Mexico could consider an approach similar to the "Palermo Model," which helped that city in Italy to successfully confront the mafia in Sicily in the 1980s and 1990s.[40] In place of a repressive law enforcement effort, this model focuses on socially based actions intended to create a culture of adherence to the rule of law. Tourists and businesses had shunned Palermo because the mafia had completely corrupted and controlled the public sphere. Rather than fight violence and mafia lawlessness through direct attacks by law enforcement, the city's mayor, Leoluca Orlando, worked to change the culture of impunity. Based on the belief that the mafia was an inevitable part of life in that area, the mayor worked to strengthen the judiciary and address the social pressures that lead youth to become involved in illegal activities. He helped create employment and promoted civic participation, including the boycotting of businesses that continued to pay "protection" and did not stand up to the mafia. The mayor highlighted that institutional reforms would not be successful without a culture in which obeisance to the law was the norm. Accordingly, he worked through the schools, mass media, centers of moral authority, and the police to educate and spread information on the rule of law. Palermo did eventually create a "rule of law" culture and a vibrant, empowered civil society in which the mafia—although it still exists—no longer controls the mechanisms of local government.

Prominent statesmen, including former Mexican President Ernesto Zedillo and his colleagues, Fernando Henrique Cardoso of Brazil and Cesar Gaviria from Colombia, have called for the legalization of

40 Leoluca Orlando, "Fighting the Mafia and Renewing Sicilian Culture," 2001.

25

marijuana; Cardoso later advocated legalization of cocaine.[41] In August 2010 even President Calderón called for a debate on the subject of legalization, noting that in a democracy it is important to analyze the pros and cons of a wide range of opinions. Four days later, former Mexican President Vicente Fox issued a demand for the legalization of the production, sale, and distribution of all drugs.[42] On his blog, Fox wrote that legalization would not mean that drugs were good. Rather, he highlighted that legalization could be a strategy to strike and break the economic structure that allows mafias to generate huge profits in businesses that serve to corrupt the public sphere and increase their own power. The objective underlying any legalization strategy would be to gain control over the enormous profits the TCOs gain through their illicit sale of drugs.

Decriminalization is a somewhat similar approach, which would entail removing criminal penalties for the possession or personal consumption of quantities of certain drugs under a small, stipulated limit. Last year, Mexico decriminalized small quantities of marijuana, although cocaine could also be included in a decriminalization plan. The logic underpinning such a strategy holds that by decriminalizing the possession of small quantities of marijuana, the police could more efficiently concentrate their efforts on more egregious crimes such as the production, trafficking, and sale of drugs like cocaine, which would remain illegal.

2). Impact on US/Mexico Defense Relationship.

The shift from a strategy of confronting organized crime in Mexico to a socially based alternative approach could significantly impact the current level of US/Mexican defense relations. One key in determining how great that impact would be involves whether Mexico would choose to engage in a socially based alternative with or *without* a law enforcement component aimed at confronting organized criminal organizations.

It is noteworthy that the city of Palermo's campaign against the mafia did not emphasize a repressive or confrontational effort against the mafia; however, the federal government of Italy did. So, to portray the success of the Palermo Model solely on the merits of its socially focused efforts would be somewhat disingenuous. In a somewhat analogous situation, President Álvaro Uribe's highly successful "Democratic Security" strategy in Colombia did include extensive emphasis on social programs. However, these programs were integrated into a strategy whose principal objective was to dismantle and destroy the major drug cartels.[43] Accordingly, a major part of Colombia's success during the Uribe years was based on the foundation of security achieved through the strong military and police component of that strategy.[44]

41 "Ex-presidents of Latin America urge legal marijuana," CNN, February 11, 2009.
http://www.cnn.com/2009/WORLD/americas/02/11/brazil marijuana/index.html?iref=allsearch.
42 "Mexico and Drugs: Thinking the Unthinkable," *The Economist*, August 14, 2010, pp. 28-29.
43 Robert C. Bonner, "The New Cocaine Cowboys: How to Defeat Mexico's Drug Cartels," *Foreign Affairs* (July/August 2010), pp. 38, 42.
44 CHDS Colombia study, pre-publication draft, March 2011.

26

July 2011 Volume 1 Number 1
Strategic Issues in U.S.-Latin American Relations
Critical Strategic Decisions in Mexico: the Future of US/Mexican Defense Relations

If the next presidential administration in Mexico chooses a socially based alternative that does not include a confrontational component against the TCOs, the Mexican military would in all likelihood return to its traditional missions. As the approaches covered within this option emphasize a more social and cultural programs, the police would take the lead role. In such a scenario, the military would probably return to its traditional defense and security missions, thus reducing the need for cooperation with US military and defense counterparts. US relations with the Mexican Navy would most likely continue because of the range of interaction that these forces maintain regarding international and sea border engagement, exercises, and so on. However, the Army would probably retake its more insular focus on internal security and external defense. The United States could once again play the role of the potential enemy against which the Mexican Army must defend from another potential intervention in its homeland.[45] Over time the US/Mexico defense relationship could easily revert to its pre-Calderón state, with polite, but distant, relations.

On the other hand, the next administration could choose a socially based strategy that includes a more traditional law enforcement–focused campaign against organized crime. If so, the Mexican military could continue to support the police in a manner generally consistent with the situation described in the post-transitional phase of Option B. The crucial difference would hinge on whether that strategy entailed continued Mexican military support to the police in confronting the TCOs. If so, that scenario could yield sustained sharing of intelligence, logistical, and operational support, as well as experience in coordinating federal, state, and local agencies and other organizations. Given this situation, the US/Mexican defense relationship could very well continue along the lines discussed in Option B.

Option D. Adopt a Strategy to Tacitly Accommodate or Negotiate Directly with TCOs

1). Discussion of Option.

This option offers a scenario in which the next administration chooses to reject direct confrontation with the TCOs. The objective of such a strategy would be to reduce or eliminate violence in Mexico resulting from conflict among the cartels or between the TCOs and government security forces. The modality would be government negotiation or accommodation with the TCOs. Implicit within that approach (most likely without publicly stating its intentions), the government would avoid cooperating with the United States to repress the cartels. Such accommodation could be accomplished tacitly. Or, in the worst of cases, the government might directly or indirectly broker agreements defining geographi-

---

45 Nevertheless, personal relationships may serve as a mitigating factor. A significant number of Mexican military personnel would have established positive contacts over a period of years with members of a US military force they had early in their careers considered enemies. For many Mexican soldiers, those personal contacts could be a catalyst in reducing the stigma of interacting with US military forces. That said, those relationships are likely to diminish over time unless they have been institutionalized or sustained through the establishment of agreements, organization, or other means.

27

July 2011 Volume 1 Number 1
Strategic Issues in U.S.-Latin American Relations
Critical Strategic Decisions in Mexico: the Future of US/Mexican Defense Relations

cal trafficking corridors to the United States for each cartel. Under this type of arrangement, the cartels could continue their drug trafficking business focused on the US market without concern for confrontation with government security forces unless their failure to honor their tacit or formal agreements caused problems inside Mexico.

This type of accommodation scenario may seem far-fetched. However, during its 70 years in power, the PRI maintained stability and avoided party fragmentation through a corporatist approach. The PRI would essentially "buy off" dissidents with jobs, programs, subsidies, sinecures, or other incentives to appease their complaints and thereby incorporate these potentially problematic individuals and groups into the political system. Within that framework, the PRI allowed major drug cartels to increase their influence and power, due partially to entrenched corruption and a lack of accountability within the government.[46] Examples of such high-level corruption abound. In the 1980s, the entire Federal Security Directorate was disbanded because it had been completely taken over by the drug cartels.[47] Another well-known instance in 1998 involved President Ernesto Zedillo's Drug Czar, General Jesús Gutiérrez Rebollo. Although praised by his US counterpart Barry McCaffrey for his integrity, General Gutiérrez was arrested barely two months later for having been on the Juarez Cartel payroll for years. Moreover, while the federal police lacked the skills and authority necessary to carry out investigations, criminal organizations controlled the state and municipal police. As a result, the Mexican government could not act effectively against the cartels even when the political will to do so existed.[48]

In this vein, two former senior Mexican officials, Jorge Casteñeda and Ruben Águilar, have expressed a worrisome perspective. They stated publicly that Mexico's war on drugs and organized crime has failed—and cannot be won.[49] Moreover, they highlight that the drug problem is only an issue for the United States—not for Mexico. The authors assert that since the United States is not willing to address the drug war effectively, Mexicans could reduce violence in their country by, in effect, tolerating narcotics-trafficking organizations. They emphasize that it is not necessary to have an explicit pact with the TCOs; moreover, tacit agreements with the TCOs regarding drugs would allow Mexican security forces to concentrate on citizen security tasks such as extortion, kidnapping, and theft.

Further, some commentators assert that a PRI victory in the presidential election would in effect bring about the adoption of option D.[50] Perhaps such assertions are partisan efforts to curry votes for other political parties.[51] Or, they may reflect concern that 12 years out of office may be insufficient time for

---

46 Bonner, p. 38.
47 Jorge Castañeda, "What's Spanish for Quagmire?" *Foreign Policy*, January/February 2010, p. 80.
48 Bonner, p. 39.
49 Ruben Aguilar V. and Jorge Castañeda.
50 Denise Dresser, "What's the Matter with Mexico: Drugs, Dinosaurs, Dithering," presentation at the Mexico Institute, Woodrow Wilson International Center for Scholars, Washington DC, April 2011, pp. 4-5.
51 Stratfor, "New Mexican President, Same Cartel War?" http://www.stratfor.com/weekly/20110614-new-Mexican-president-same-cartel-war? ip_auth_redirect=1, June 14, 2011.

28

July 2011 Volume 1 Number 1
Strategic Issues in U.S.-Latin American Relations
Critical Strategic Decisions in Mexico: the Future of US/Mexican Defense Relations

the PRI to have transformed the party "machinery" and developed over 70 years in power.

Whatever the motivation, the adoption of Option B could be quite problematic for Mexico. Within the context of an effective democratic society, the drawbacks of such an option would entail a dramatic increase in impunity, making a mockery of the rule of law and fostering a culture of lawlessness. Further, an accommodation strategy may be more difficult to achieve than Casteñeda and Águilar assert. The structure and sheer numbers of modern TCOs would make the old "PRI-style" arrangements much more difficult to enforce. Moreover, the TCOs have expanded their malicious portfolios beyond drugs; crimes such as kidnapping and extortion are now integral to their overall operations. Would the TCOs simply give up their pervasive and lucrative business networks to concentrate only on drugs shipments to the United States?

2). Impact on US/Mexico Defense Relationship.

From the perspective of improving US/Mexican defense relations, Option D would be the worst possible outcome. Whether a Mexican government's willingness to negotiate directly with the TCOs stemmed from corruption at the highest levels, institutional weakness, or simply an effort to reduce violence in Mexico, the impact would be devastating to US/Mexican security and defense cooperation. In such a case, positive relations with the US military would be inconvenient for the Mexican government. So if the next administration chose a strategy of TCO accommodation, the Mexican government would undoubtedly seek to halt all activities between US and Mexican military and defense counterparts, and try to dismantle any existing institutional linkages. In this scenario, the administration would most likely order the Mexican military to focus solely on its traditional missions and stop supporting law enforcement operations, which would place the military at odds with the TCOs. Whereas President Calderón's order to the military to work with their US counterparts resulted in greatly improved cooperation, a presidential order to halt any relations with the United States would have detrimental consequences for further collaboration.[52]

Under such conditions the United States would seek to maintain institutional military-to-military ties while awaiting the return of a government that would confront the TCOs. Cooperation would no doubt be limited, at best, to functional connections such as disaster relief and border coordination issues. During that "sexenio," the United States would clearly be unwilling to pass information or intelligence to Mexico for fear that such information would be passed almost immediately to the TCOs. The Mexican military would presumably return to its traditional mission to defend against the improbable threat of a US invasion.

---

52 Institutional relationships can be cut more abruptly. However, given the proliferation of social media outlets such as Facebook and Twitter, it is harder to cut off personal relations that have already been established among individuals.

29

Summary of Options to Counter TCO Threats

Options	Option A: Military in Lead Role	Option B: Law Enforcement Lead Role vs. TCOs	Option C: Socially based Alternatives	Option D: Accommodation/Negotiation with TCOs
Description	• Continuation of Calderón administration's strategy with military lead in the fight vs. TCOs	• Transfer lead responsibility of fighting the TCOs from the military to the police	• Focus on social programs that promote a "culture of lawfulness"	• Tacit approval of or direct negotiations w/TCOs to allow conduct of illicit trafficking activities
Advantages	• Maintains focus on reducing corruption/impunity	• Offers opportunity to announce new strategy/fresh start. • Law enforcement is appropriate institution to lead fight vs. TCOs	• City of Palermo achieved success vs mafia with a socially focused approach.	• Strategy could reduce currently high levels of TCO violence
Disadvantages	• Popular support for current strategy is decreasing	• Police reforms necessary for effective transfer of lead role will take years	• Socially based approaches may require a law enforcement component to achieve success	• Institutionalizes culture of impunity—makes sham of "rule of law" efforts
Potential Outcome for US/Mexico Defense Relations	• Continued improvement in cooperation and collaboration	• The greater the military's support of the police, the more cooperation between US and Mexican militaries	• Dependent on whether Mexico includes/does not include law enforcement component	• Severely limits/ends cooperation achieved during Calderón administration

July 2011 Volume 1 Number 1
Strategic Issues in U.S.-Latin American Relations
Critical Strategic Decisions in Mexico: the Future of US/Mexican Defense Relations

4. Recommendations.

Once elected, the next government in Mexico will wrestle with the practical decision of how to confront the TCOs. The result may or may not match positions stated during the electoral campaign. However, the strategy chosen is likely to fall within the range of the four options described above. Each option offers vastly different considerations. From a US policy perspective, a Mexican strategy that fosters continuation of US/Mexican cooperation and collaboration established during the Calderón administration would be the most desirable. Options A ("Stay the Course") and B ("Law Enforcement vs. Military Lead") would be most compatible with current US efforts to address the TCO threat. Option C ("Socially Focused Alternatives") could also be consistent with current bilateral forms of security collaboration—as long as Mexico retains an integrated a counter-TCO component along with social approaches to create a culture of lawfulness. However, if the Mexican government chooses Option D ("Accommodate the TCOs"), the United States would be forced to seriously consider restricting all forms of functional cooperation involving sensitive information and intelligence. The impact of that policy choice would reverse the collaboration and cooperation developed over the past several years.

The US/Mexican defense relationship has evolved into a visible bellwether for the level of the two nations' commitment and joint efforts to confront the TCOs. Early in his administration, President Calderón made unprecedented decisions to reach out to the United States to work together to confront the TCOs and to place the Mexican military in the lead role in that fight. One consequence was that the US/Mexican defense relationship became an important and visible aspect of each nation's combined struggle against organized crime. Despite that historically significant opportunity and the improvements in the military-to-military relationship it engendered, the US, as a nation, did not respond convincingly to Mexico's effort to confront transnational criminal organizations. The U.S. Congress did approve aid for Mexico in the Mérida Initiative, and US leaders praised President Calderón's courageous decision to address organized crime. Yet the slow, bureaucratic release of that aid made the US commitment appear halfhearted and unresponsive. If the United States wants the next government in Mexico to be a strong partner in this effort, we must show in deeds, not words, that we are committed to partnership.

So, what can the United States do to encourage Mexico to make strategic choices facilitating the continued collaboration and improved defense relationships necessary to confront the TCO threat? First, the United States must demonstrate commitment to serving as a dedicated partner and show its willingness to assist the next government in Mexico in combating organized crime with the same or even greater levels of effort. That approach demands substantive support for the efforts of Mexican military and public security forces as tangible evidence of US solidarity. Second, the United States and Mexico must have a solid understanding regarding how the two countries can work together, while addressing domestic political realities. Third, those who influence policy in both Mexico and the United States

31

must seek to galvanize pressure on key actors in Congress and the media toward favorable approaches and actions that will assist our mutual efforts in successfully confronting the TCOs.[53] Given the importance of achieving those ends, the following recommendations are offered to help improve military-to-military and defense relations among the two countries and mitigate the impact of potentially negative future political decisions.

Demonstrate Success during a Rapidly Closing "Window of Opportunity."

The United States should assist the Calderón administration wherever necessary, and possible, to achieve visible, tangible success in disrupting and countering TCO operations. Moreover, such US assistance should avoid any semblance of encroachment of Mexican sovereignty. There is a rapidly closing "window" of time while the administration remains in office. A major factor in the next president's assessment of whether to "stay the course" or seek dramatic change may be the perceived level of success the Calderón administration achieves in confronting organized crime. If Calderón's efforts appear successful in reducing the TCOs' ability to carry out violence and illicit activities, a government of any party will have an incentive to maintain that positive momentum toward greater rule of law. The choice would be easier for an elected PAN administration, which could highlight the need for continuity of effort and perhaps seek to benefit from some of the luster of the Calderón administration's success. On the other hand, if the nation perceives the cartels are winning, the next administration could readily declare the previous administration's policy a failure and seek a radical change of strategy. Even an incoming PAN administration may find it difficult to maintain a confrontational approach against the TCOs if the Calderón administration's efforts are widely viewed as failed.

Facilitate Strategies and Actions That Offer Continuity in Enhancing the US/Mexico Defense Relationship.

Our bias should favor arrangements that allow US and Mexican military forces to continue to work together on as wide a range of functional and operational areas as possible. The longer that US and Mexican military personal and units work together, the greater the probability they will develop standard operating procedures and common tactics, techniques, and procedures to make our combined efforts more effective. Although US citizens are generally unaware that Mexicans feel a national sense of indignation toward the United States, the Mexican military has long maintained a professional culture that kept its distance and was reluctant to engage with its US counterparts beyond a limited basis. In other words, from the Mexican perspective we have an eventful history to overcome. The longer that US and Mexican military counterparts work together and sustain personal and professional relationships, the greater the likelihood that we can chip away at those animosities.

---

53 Erik Kjonnerod has highlighted that Israeli-American and Cuban-American groups offer useful examples in this regard.

32

July 2011 Volume 1 Number 1
Strategic Issues in U.S.-Latin American Relations
Critical Strategic Decisions in Mexico: the Future of US/Mexican Defense Relations

Expand and Institutionalize Existing US/Mexico Defense Linkages and Organizational Arrangements.

Experience has shown that institutionalized, positive US/Mexican defense relationships established during past warming trends tended to fade away when the personalities involved retired or were reassigned. The United States should seek to create and expand operational and organizational linkages while we enjoy relatively favorable defense relations. We should specifically seek to institutionalize advancements in US/Mexican defense relations achieved during the Calderón administration. Once formally established, signed agreements, international boards, and combined units and organizations are more difficult to dismantle. Such institutionalized arrangements help mitigate and dampen the impact of changes resulting from political transitions. As previously mentioned, a lofty, long-term goal toward which we should focus is the establishment of a bi-national or even tri-national (Mexico, US, Canada) command in Mexico under Mexican civilian or military leadership. This institution could address humanitarian and disaster-relief issues, protection of critical infrastructure, cyber security, intelligence sharing, or other mutually beneficial areas of mutual interest. Even if a government that is opposed to closer US/Mexican defense ties takes power, it may take a consistent effort over time to decrease the value and importance of an existing network of agreements and coordination and assistance protocols.

Coordinate a Comprehensive US Strategy That Integrates with and Demonstrates Solidarity and Support for Mexican Efforts to Confront Organized Crime.

Given the transnational nature of organized crime, we recognize that the United States cannot address this issue without the help and involvement of international partners. Accordingly, we must ensure that we stand united against this threat with our southern neighbor. If we want Mexico to be willing to work with the United States in this fight, we must develop the political conditions that will indeed make Mexico want to work with us. The three-year Mérida Initiative support is ending. The United States should work with Mexico to develop and establish a follow-up strategy that demonstrates US resolve and leverages all instruments of national power to help address Mexico's security problems effectively.

A bi-national initiative with the full support of both nations will be required to achieve success against powerful and agile transnational criminal organizations—a possible, but very difficult, task to accomplish in either, let alone both, countries. US programs should continue to focus on building much needed judicial, intelligence, and law enforcement capacity in Mexico.

Identify Realistically Attainable Objectives and Manage Expectations.

We must work with Mexico to determine realistic objectives that can be accomplished through a bi-

33

national partnership. Mexico's domestic political issues are as complicated and as difficult as our own. On the one hand, the United States would have Mexico accomplish judicial, law enforcement, and legislative reforms that would make their efforts against the TCOs more effective. However, in Mexico all these issues have proven the most controversial and problematic to achieve. Conversely, the Mexicans expect the United States to achieve the political objectives they desire. For example, at every opportunity, Mexican officials ask the United States to do more to reduce demand for drugs, and to control the flow of weapons and cash from the United States to Mexican TCOs. Indeed, a prominent Mexican legislator recently complained publicly that all Mexican Army checkpoints searching for drugs headed north should be turned around to check for weapons and cash headed south.[54] Yet the issues most important to Mexico, such as gun control and immigration reform, are the most controversial, painful, and divisive for the United States.

Bell-412 Helicopter formal delivery ceremony in the SEDENA Hanger at Benito Juarez International Airport Mexico City December 15 2009 which marked the official handover of five helicopters to the government of Mexico under the Merida Initiative.

Over the past several years, the improving US/Mexican defense relationship has been an important indicator of the commitment our nations give to a combined effort to fight transnational organized crime. The United States should seek to maintain the momentum and bilateral collaboration this key aspect entails. Those in Mexico who oppose a strategy to confront the TCOs assert that the United States is not taking the actions necessary to assist Mexico solve its problems. In many ways these crit-

54 Conference at the Mexican Naval War College (Centro de Estudios Superiores Navales [CESNAV]), Mexico City, Mexico, April 2011.

34

July 2011 Volume 1 Number 1
Strategic Issues in U.S.-Latin American Relations
Critical Strategic Decisions in Mexico: the Future of US/Mexican Defense Relations

ics are right. Achieving a US strategy that would truly support Mexico is difficult because it demands consensus from influential domestic interest groups. To accomplish their political agendas, these groups do not necessarily intend to scapegoat Mexico. But the collective result can be a US policy or program that does not demonstrate the appropriate urgency or solidarity with Mexico on challenges that affect the United States. Such a plurality of views results in a lackluster effort in providing effective assistance. More importantly, it emphasizes to our Mexican neighbors that too few in the United States recognize or even care that the stakes are high in Mexico. The US/Mexican defense relationship is a demonstrable, unifying element toward confronting our shared security challenges. We still have the opportunity to shape conditions that may determine Mexico's strategic decisions on how to address organized crime and violence. The time to take action to demonstrate US resolve in this fight so critical to US interests is now ■

35

July 2011 Volume 1 Number 1
Strategic Issues in U.S.-Latin American Relations
Critical Strategic Decisions in Mexico: the Future of US/Mexican Defense Relations